KICK START YOUR TEEN'S CAREER EXPLORATION

GAIN CAREER COACHING KNOWLEDGE AND EMPOWER YOUR TEEN WITH QUICK, EASY ACTIVITIES TO FIND CAREER DIRECTION

AMY ZDANOWSKI

Good Dog Publishing

Copyright © 2024 AmyZ Career Guidance

All rights reserved. This book is protected. You may not copy or use any part of this book without permission from the Author or publisher. This book is for learning, assistance, and entertainment; it is not intended to be legal, financial, medical, or other professional advice. The information contained in this book is as accurate as possible at the time of print. The Author and publisher are not responsible for any issues or problems you might have from the info in the book.

This book is only for personal use - direct requests for other uses to amyzcareerguidance@yahoo.com.

ISBN 979-8-9895067-0-5

Cover design by: Cubist, 99Designs.com

Good Dog Publishing

Producing content that is enjoyable and reliable, much like a "good dog."

CONTENTS

Introduction	5
1. FROM DREAMS TO REALITY	9
The One Perfect Job Myth	9
Childhood Dreams: Clues To Future Careers	11
"What's Your Plan After High School?" A Loaded Question	13
Questions to Ponder	15
2. UNDERSTANDING WORK STYLE PREFERENCES	17
THE WORK STYLE PREFERENCES	19
WORK STYLE PREFERENCES IN ACTION	21
QUESTIONS TO PONDER	24
3. HOW INTERESTS INFORM CAREER EXPLORATION	25
THE SIX CAREER TYPES	26
4. YOUR TEEN'S INPUT	31
TEEN ACTIVITIES to COMPLETE	32
5. PROCESSING YOUR TEEN'S INPUT	39
6. CAREER TYPE PROFILES	45
R - Realistic (Doers)	46
I - Investigative (Explorers)	47
A - Artistic (Creators)	48
S - Social (Helpers)	49
E - Enterprising (Motivators)	50
C - Conventional (Organizers)	51
7. CAREER TYPES IN ACTION	53
8. GUIDING YOUR TEEN INTO ACTION	59
A Closing Message To Parents	63
References	67

INTRODUCTION

Congratulations! You are about to help your teen transition from feeling undecided or uncertain to confidently declaring, "I have a direction!"

In this book, you'll take on the crucial role of guiding your teen to discover their career identity and promising career sectors to explore. Together, we'll delve into understanding your teen's Career Type and Work Style Preference, unlocking valuable insights to illuminate their path forward.

This book is not an exhaustive A-to-Z guide on career planning. It's tailored for parents facing the unique challenge of helping teens who are either undecided about a career path, feel overwhelmed by too many options, or are so engrossed in the present that they have not contemplated the future. This book is crafted with these teens in mind, providing you with the tools to kick start their career exploration journey.

We understand that life is hectic, and parents of teens have limited time to spare. This book is intentionally concise, focusing on two essential aspects of the career planning process that have consistently guided teens toward meaningful futures. The chapters are short to accommodate small windows of time to read, but they also flow nicely and can be completed relatively quickly.

In the following pages, you will learn two fundamental concepts in career coaching: Work Style Preferences and Career Types. As you embark on this journey with us, we aim to furnish you with practical strategies and empower you with the rationale behind these career coaching methods, enabling you to support your teen effectively. We've created a few short activities specifically tailored for your teen, accompanied by guidance on interpreting and making the most of the insights gained.

While this book applies to individuals of all ages, we focus on helping teens nearing the end of high school or recently graduated. Let's embark on this journey together and guide your teen toward a future brimming with potential and purpose.

Having spent over two decades as a school counselor and currently serving as a college career advisor, I've been privileged to guide thousands of students on their path to a meaningful future. Throughout my career, a simple yet powerful motto has emerged: Explore. Plan. Do.

You see, some teens have no trouble dreaming about their future. They envision the adventures they'll embark upon, the places they'll call home, the income they'll earn, and the lives they'll positively influence. Some even make plans to achieve their goals. Yet, all too often, these plans never see action. This book is your tool to bridge that gap and guide your teen into action.

To truly benefit from the wisdom contained within these pages, it's essential that both you and your teen actively participate in the discussions and exercises provided. This is not just a book of advice; it's a journey with a purpose, and your role as the tour guide is paramount.

Together, we will help your teen navigate the maze of career options, empowering them with a deeper understanding of themselves and how that relates to career choices, training, and overall career satisfaction.

Your time is valuable. Every activity in this book serves a specific purpose, even if the connection isn't immediately apparent, so we urge you to complete all activities. We've also included note pages in the back for you to jot down insights, questions, and thoughts for your teen as they arise.

Now, with enthusiasm and commitment, let's get started.

CHAPTER 1
FROM DREAMS TO REALITY

THE ONE PERFECT JOB MYTH

Meet Sarah, a high school senior full of dreams and a bundle of aspirations. Like many teens, she often heard well-intentioned advice such as, "Find your passion," or, "Do what you love, and work will never feel like work." She embarked on her journey to find that one perfect job that would encapsulate all her dreams and desires, but little did she know the path was filled with twists and turns.

In the pursuit of guiding teens like Sarah toward fulfilling careers, we must address "find your passion." Such phrases can inadvertently lead our teens to believe that there is only one dream career out there waiting for them, and it's their sole mission to discover it. This notion of a single ideal career match can be overwhelming and discouraging. Often, students like Sarah are eager to leap to the finish line and pick a job title without truly understanding themselves, their motivations, sources of energy, and their values.

To help our teens break free from the "one perfect job" mindset, let's consider what people say when asked what they love about their careers:

- "I love my job because I get to help people."
- "I love my job because I can be creative."
- "I love my job because it fits great with being a parent."
- "I love my job because it challenges me."
- "I love my job because of the people I work with."

You see, fulfilling careers are usually tied to a value, a task, a feeling, or an outcome. As parents, you can help your teen grasp this concept and see that every job has highs and lows. It's entirely normal to have aspects of a job you might not enjoy. Disliking certain elements of your job doesn't equate to failure; it's simply a part of reality. Teens don't always realize this, and during their research, they often eliminate a career possibility because of one task they think they wouldn't like.

Imagine the career exploration journey as a funnel, with its wide opening at the top. At this initial stage, our primary focus is to help teens discover and embrace their unique qualities and preferences. We're laying the foundation, helping them understand who they are, what drives them, and what excites them about the world of work.

As teens progress through the funnel, it gradually narrows, representing the transition from self-discovery to eventual career selection and preparation. We are at the top of the funnel and just getting started, so it's important to remind your teen they need not be overwhelmed by details. This early stage is about broadening horizons, understanding their Career Types, and identifying their Work Style Preferences.

Our goal is not to pigeonhole them into a specific job title prematurely but to pinpoint the broad career sectors and fields that resonate with their interests and natural tendencies. This approach empowers them to embark on their career exploration journey with purpose and enthusiasm, paving the way for a fulfilling and successful future.

Remember, you're not alone on this journey. Encourage your teen, share your experiences, and keep the lines of communication open. Together, we'll navigate the world of career possibilities, one step at a time.

CHILDHOOD DREAMS: CLUES TO FUTURE CAREERS

A helpful way to begin their career exploration journey is to tap into their childhood dreams. From a young age, children are often asked, "What do you want to be when you grow up?" It's a simple question, but the answers can reveal a lot about their personalities, values, and motivations. These dreams may seem whimsical, but they can serve as valuable clues in the career exploration journey.

Ask your teen about careers they dreamed of when they were little. Some will know immediately; others might need a little prompting from you. Take the time to talk about what they thought they'd like about the careers they dreamed of when they were little. Even if what they wanted to be was completely unique or even made-up, explore that. Something motivated them to think, "I'd like to do this."

Please take note of what they say. Career dreams of our younger days often develop from a few common themes. Sometimes, the career is familiar to them: careers of parents, family friends, friend's parents, and people they are exposed to regularly. Other times, it's based on their experiences or books they read. Maybe it's what their best friend wants to be, so they want to be that, too. Perhaps due to requiring specialized medical care, they develop a deep admiration for the healthcare professionals who aided in their recovery. This newfound inspiration may lead them to set their sights on a future path in the same field. Regardless of the reason, revisiting their early career dreams is a great place to find clues to their developing nature and motivators.

For example, let's say a child dreamed of being an astronaut. What might this tell us? Perhaps this child values exploration and adventure and is motivated by discovering new things and pushing boundaries.

Let's consider what a few other childhood dreams might reveal about your teen:

The Future Firefighter: Children with this dream may be drawn to being a hero, protecting people, and making a difference during emergencies. This dream underscores the values of bravery, responsibility, and a sense of adventure.

The Fairy Princess: Consider the dream of being a princess. This dream often underscores a love for imagination, kindness, and compassion. It speaks to a sense of wonder and an appreciation for beauty in the world.

The Pro Athlete in the Making: For those who dreamt of being a professional athlete, it may signify a competitive nature, a love for physical activity, or a desire to be recognized for their skills. This dream often points to an appreciation for goal setting and teamwork.

The Aspiring Veterinarian: This one can be complicated. Animal lovers often aspire to be veterinarians because that's a career with animals familiar to them. Many aspiring veterinarians eventually discover that what they love is the relationship, interaction, and connection with animals instead of the science and function of animals. Early career dreams of being a veterinarian often indicate a caring, helpful child who values relationships.

To kick start a meaningful conversation with your teen:

1. Sit down together and revisit their childhood dreams.
2. Encourage them to share their aspirations and the reasons behind those dreams.
3. Take this opportunity to share *your* childhood dreams and how they may have shaped your values and interests.

This dialogue is a powerful starting point for understanding your teen's aspirations and guiding them in their career exploration journey.

"WHAT'S YOUR PLAN AFTER HIGH SCHOOL?" A LOADED QUESTION

The seemingly innocent question, "What's your plan after high school?" can weigh heavily on students' minds. The expectation of having a clear and decisive answer to this question can be overwhelming, leading to uncertainty and anxiety. Graduating students often struggle to make definitive choices about their future.

To the parents reading this book, consider this: many of you may have had one plan in mind as you approached the end of high school, only to find yourselves pursuing entirely different paths today. This is not a failure; it's a testament to growth and change. Students must remember that the careers they see adults in today are often not the result of a straight and narrow path.

Let me share my journey as an example. In my hometown, it was customary for students to create a memory book during their final year of high school—a keepsake filled with memories, photos, and plans for the future. I still have that book, and the last page outlines my plan after high school: I aimed to attend college, earn a bachelor's degree in criminal justice, and work for the federal government. I attended college, earned that degree, and even received a job offer from the United States Marshal Service. However, I decided to turn down that job offer.

In high school, I was drawn to concepts like rules, justice, fairness, and helping others, which led me to pursue a degree in criminal justice. Throughout my college studies, I delved deeper into the workings of the U.S. criminal justice system as well as my motivations and values. I learned that the system often operates reactively, responding to behavior after it has already occurred and striving to change behaviors to prevent further encounters with the criminal justice system.

However, I had an epiphany—I felt compelled to take a proactive approach instead. Rather than working within the existing criminal justice system, I wanted to focus on preventing individuals from entering the system in the first place. I believed by assisting people before they ventured into criminal activities, I could make a more profound and lasting impact on my community. My degree and motivation to adopt this proactive stance led me to my first job, working with youth.

Careers evolve and change over time, often taking unexpected twists and turns. Students frequently perceive the path from high school to a career as a straight trajectory. The question, "What do you want to be?" often reinforces this notion. While it's a seemingly simple question, it carries considerable weight for students nearing the end of their high school education.

Rather than pressuring students to define their future careers, we can help them explore their options, rule out specific paths, and narrow down their choices. By guiding your teen to identify their strengths, interests, and natural abilities, they can feel more confident and motivated to make informed decisions about their next steps.

As parents actively engaged in this journey alongside our teens, it's essential to reflect on how we perceive our teens and consider potential career choices worth exploring. Yes, ultimately, they will decide for themselves. But our teens often don't recognize some of the strengths and natural abilities we have watched them develop over the years, which makes parental input needed and valuable.

QUESTIONS TO PONDER

1. What are five words describing your teen?
2. Are there specific careers or fields you believe your teen is well-suited for and should consider? If so, list them and note why they may be a good fit.
3. What types of careers are unlikely to be a good fit for your teen and why?

CHAPTER 2
UNDERSTANDING WORK STYLE PREFERENCES

This chapter focuses on how parents can support their teens in the career exploration process by identifying and understanding work style preferences. By gaining insights into these preferences, parents can effectively guide their teens in narrowing down careers to explore. Have you ever noticed that people seem happiest when their work aligns with their natural abilities and inclinations? Think about your teen for a moment. Do they have a strong desire to help others, a knack for organizing things, a flair for creativity, or a talent for working with their hands? These are all clues as to your teen's Work Style.

Imagine that all careers can be neatly sorted into four distinctive styles. Instead of navigating a daunting maze of countless careers, picture having a reliable compass as a guide. This compass, called "Work Styles," has been a game changer for many teens, propelling them into their career exploration journey with confidence and clarity.

Work Styles are based on what a person prefers to work with naturally. Here are the four Work Styles:

- Working with PEOPLE.
- Working with DATA
- Working with THINGS
- Working with IDEAS

Before we delve into your teen's preferences regarding Work Styles, let's understand why they matter. Knowing how you are wired and what types of activities or tasks you prefer can be a great starting point for career exploration. Work Styles can be seen in how people interact with others, in their hobbies, and even in situations that cause anxiety or joy. Here is a story that illustrates how Work Styles appear even when we are young.

At the neighborhood park, a group of children were engrossed in a lively game of tag. They darted around, chasing and evading one another. During the game, one child suddenly fell and twisted his ankle, wincing in pain. Emily, known for her concern for others, immediately halted the game and rushed to the boy's side. She helped him to his feet, offered comforting words, and suggested they move to the side of the playing field.

Murphy, an active, practical boy, also noticed the fall. However, his reaction was different. He paused briefly and watched Emily help the fallen boy. Once he saw that the injured boy was in good hands, Murphy took action in his own way. With a nod to the rest of the friends, who had stopped playing due to the incident, Murphy announced, "Okay, let's get back to the game." He swiftly resumed the chase, leading others to rejoin the fun.

This simple park scenario displays the contrasting Work Styles of PEOPLE and THINGS. Emily's consistent concern for others points to her natural inclination toward PEOPLE. Murphy's desire to resume the game and be active indicates a natural tendency toward doing and working with THINGS.

Moments like this show how Work Styles are displayed from a young age in everyday situations. They reflect our natural tendencies and extend far beyond career choices. Work Styles show in our hobbies, actions, reactions, and more. They aren't just theoretical concepts; they are practical tools that empower teenagers to understand themselves better and make informed decisions about their future.

In the first chapter, we discussed what people love about their work. Remember the phrases "I get to help people," "I get to work with my hands," or "I solve problems"? These phrases often reflect an individual's Work Style. That's why we believe it's essential to spend time helping teens understand how they are naturally wired rather than simply discussing available careers. Once a teen identifies their Work Style, a common strategy is to have them Google careers that fit that work style or a combination of two styles.

THE WORK STYLE PREFERENCES

Now that we've introduced the concept of Work Styles let's delve deeper into the specific preferences individuals may have. Meet Alex. From a young age, he had a fascination with gadgets and machines. He eagerly took things apart and tried to reassemble them, showing an innate curiosity about how things work. Alex is the friend everyone went to when they needed help fixing their bicycle or building a treehouse. In high school, he found a home in woodworking class, crafting items that combined beauty and function. Alex is the embodiment of someone who excels in working with THINGS.

By exploring the four Work Styles, you can help your teenager pinpoint what they are naturally drawn to. Here is a deeper look at each of the four Work Styles.

The PEOPLE work style involves collaborating and interacting with others through communication, guidance, service, or teamwork. Occupations within this category often encompass roles such as providing customer service, ensuring safety, hospitality, education, personal guidance, and healthcare. Professions in this category require communication skills, empathy, active listening, and the ability to work effectively with others. This Work Style is about building connections and understanding human behavior while helping, coaching, guiding, or supporting individuals or groups. Does your teen excel in interpersonal skills, enjoy helping their friends through tough times, or successfully coach others? If so, they might have a PEOPLE-oriented Work Style. The PEOPLE work style is indispensable because it offers services and support that enable individuals to lead healthy, productive, and fulfilling lives.

The DATA work style revolves around managing, processing, and analyzing information. Professionals in this category harness their expertise to gather, organize, and interpret data, extracting insights, trends, and valuable information. Careers in this style may include risk analysts, statisticians, accountants, and data scientists. This work style involves roles like financial planning, analysis, research, and software development. It is the preference for those who thrive on numbers, statistics, and problem-solving. Does your teenager enjoy solving puzzles or excel in math classes? Do they have a fascination with understanding patterns and drawing conclusions from information? If so, they might have a DATA-oriented Work Style. The DATA work style plays a pivotal role in businesses and organizations as they gather vast amounts of information and formulate valuable insights and actions based on data.

Next is the THINGS work style. This revolves around the physical world and tangible aspects of life. It encompasses manufacturing, construction, agriculture, and maintenance, including electricians, plumbers, and mechanics. Roles within this category demand technical skills and the physical ability to work with equipment, machinery, tools, and objects. This style focuses on building, fixing, or maintaining things and understanding how gadgets and machines work. Does your teenager enjoy hands-on activities or show an interest in the mechanics of everyday items? If so, they might have a THINGS-oriented Work Style. This work style is vital because it is responsible for producing the physical goods and structures that form the foundation of our daily lives, including food and shelter.

Last is the IDEAS work style. This work style embodies innovative thinking, exploration, and intellectual creativity, spanning the realms of artistry and analysis. It encompasses careers involving artistic expression, such as writing, graphic design, filmmaking, and any field valuing innovative thinking. It also extends to investigative roles, where professionals delve into research, problem-solving, and the generation of new concepts. Perhaps your teenager possesses a vivid imagination, excels in creative writing, art, and drama, or consistently generates new ideas and unconventional solutions. If they exhibit a penchant for investigation, critical thinking, and analytical exploration, they might have an IDEAS-oriented Work Style. This work style drives innovation and societal progress, contributing to a wide array of inventions, products, solutions, and services that we rely upon daily.

WORK STYLE PREFERENCES IN ACTION

Some teens will ask which work style is best, but there isn't a single style that outshines the others. Here's a fictional story to illustrate how the styles complement one another. People, Data, Things, and Ideas are the four characters in the story.

Once upon a time, in a small village, there lived four friends named People, Data, Things, and Ideas. They lived together in harmony and complemented each other in their day-to-day lives. Each of them has their own unique set of skills and qualities.

One day, the village was facing a significant crisis. The crops were failing, and the villagers knew this would cause a severe food shortage. As the villagers worried about what to do, the four friends came together to find a solution.

People is the most empathetic of the group, always putting others before himself. He is excellent at connecting with others and understanding their emotions and needs. He is called the "heart" of the group because of his warm and caring personality. People listened to the villagers' concerns to understand their needs and emotions.

Data gathered information on the food shortage and the resources available in the village. She is the most analytical, always keeping track of numbers and statistics. She is excellent at managing information and keeping things organized. Because of her ability to process, analyze, and manage data, she is referred to as the "brain" of the group. With her keen analytical abilities, Data provided valuable insights that helped create a solution.

Ideas is the most imaginative, always thinking outside the box. She is excellent at generating innovative ideas and finding creative solutions. Because of her ability to think creatively, she is called the "mind" of the group. Ideas generated a list of potential solutions, including starting a community garden, trading with neighboring villages, and implementing rainwater harvesting techniques.

Things is the most practical, always getting things done. He is excellent at working with physical objects, building, and adjusting things to ensure everything works smoothly. He is called the "hands" of the group because of his mechanical ability. Things put the ideas into action to start a community garden and create a rainwater collection system.

The village overcame the food crisis with the combined efforts of People, Data, Things, and Ideas. From that day on, the four friends continued to work together to solve problems and improve the lives of the villagers. They realized their unique skills and qualities were even more powerful when they worked together. They were stronger as a team than as individuals.

This story illustrates how work styles align with different aspects of career fulfillment and societal contributions and how they shape our world overall. You'll find that in many cases, people, just like careers, combine Work Styles. Picture the work styles arranged in a circle: People, Data, Things, Ideas, and back to People. This order isn't random – it's intentional based on research and illustrates how different work styles tend to connect. Knowing this order can give us insights into how individuals might naturally lean toward specific aspects of their Work Style and how these preferences can complement or contrast in different settings.

Let's look at a real-life career example that combines dominant and secondary Work Styles.

Meet Louise, a dedicated school counselor with a dominant Work Style of PEOPLE. She thrives on helping students navigate the challenges of adolescence, offering guidance, support, and a listening ear. Louise's primary career as a school counselor aligns perfectly with her PEOPLE Work Style.

However, Louise's secondary Work Style is working with DATA. She finds balance by taking on the responsibility of creating the school's master schedule each year. In this role, Louise delves into the intricacies of data and organization. This combination allows Louise to excel in a PEOPLE career while feeding her DATA side.

QUESTIONS TO PONDER

1. What do you feel your Work Style is? If you could only choose one, do you prefer working with PEOPLE, DATA, THINGS, or IDEAS?
2. Can you think of tasks that match or conflict with your Work Style?
3. What Work Style aligns with your teen's actions, interests, and strengths? Why?

CHAPTER 3
HOW INTERESTS INFORM CAREER EXPLORATION

Have you ever wondered why some people excel in certain professions while others find the same work uninspiring? Or have you noticed that some work tasks bring you joy, fulfillment, or motivation while others are a chore? The answers to these questions often lie in understanding how our career interests and natural tendencies align with different types of work.

In this chapter, we'll focus on our second career coaching tool. Career Types, developed by psychologist John Holland, are a framework that categorizes work into six main types: Realistic, Investigative, Artistic, Social, Enterprising, and Conventional (often abbreviated as RIASEC). Career Types applied to people provide insights into the types of work environments, tasks, and responsibilities that individuals are naturally drawn to. By exploring these types, we can use natural tendencies, strengths, and preferences to guide us toward careers to explore.

A person's Career Type is often determined by using an interest inventory. An interest inventory typically consists of a series of questions designed to identify your preferences and strengths, resulting in a list of career suggestions based on your responses.

However, merely glancing at the list of suggested careers and moving on is not enough. The true value of interest inventories lies in understanding why certain suggestions are made, rather than just focusing on specific job titles to consider.

When you take the time to explore the rationale behind these suggestions and why certain careers are deemed unsuitable, you gain deeper insights into your vocational preferences. Consider, for example, the often dismissed suggestion of a sanitation worker as a potential career path for some individuals. While this suggestion may initially seem unexpected, it often stems from a person indicating they prefer hands-on work, working outside, and working independently. A sanitation worker's tasks and environment reflect these preferences.

Your teen is not obligated to pursue any suggested career or career fields. However, you'll see that by helping your teen explore the reasons behind the career suggestions, they gain a better understanding of themselves. This deeper self-awareness will provide valuable insights and help connect to potential careers. While career types are just one part of a comprehensive career exploration process, they are a wonderful way to start a career search and an easy way to initiate self-assessment and awareness.

THE SIX CAREER TYPES

The Career Type classifications are so powerful that some employers use them to optimize job fit within their organizations, resulting in increased job satisfaction, innovation, and employment longevity. Here are brief descriptions of the six types. Keep in mind that many of us exhibit a dominant Career Type, but we are all a blend of types to varying degrees.

Realistic: Practical individuals who excel in hands-on work involving physical activity and tools. Examples of careers include carpenter, mechanic, electrician, and farmer. Realistic individuals are often called "doers."

Investigative: Analytical minds that thrive on problem-solving, research, and investigation. They are curious and observant. Examples of careers include scientist, engineer, and detective. Investigative individuals are often called "explorers."

Artistic: Creative souls value self-expression, innovation, and independence. They prefer work that involves flexibility. Examples of careers include musicians, writers, actors, and designers. Artistic individuals are often called "creators."

Social: Empathetic individuals who find fulfillment in helping, supporting, or guiding others. Examples of careers include community service worker, teacher, nurse, and therapist. Social individuals are often called "helpers."

Enterprising: Motivated and persuasive individuals who excel in roles involving risk-taking and leadership. Examples of careers include salesperson, entrepreneur, manager, and public relations specialist. Enterprising individuals are often called "motivators."

Conventional: Structured and organized individuals. They excel in work, emphasizing precision and attention to detail. Examples of careers include accountant, data analyst, office manager, and librarian. Conventional individuals are often called "organizers."

To further understand how careers align with Career Types, read the following charts. Each Career Type has its own chart. You'll notice that the header lists the Career Type and the related Work Style. There are nine careers that align with each Career Type. These are just a small sample of the careers that fit into each career type. Consider the tasks and work environments associated with each career listed. You'll start to notice how the careers listed within each Career Type share common themes and characteristics.

Realistic (Doers) Prefer Things Sample Realistic Careers		
Carpenter	Firefighter	Mechanic
Baker	HVAC Technician	Plumber
Electrician	Landscaper	Welder

Investigative (Explorers) Prefer Things and Ideas Sample Investigative Careers		
Architect	Data Analyst	Psychologist
Astronomer	Detective	Researcher
Biologist	Software Developer	Scientist

Artistic (Creators) Prefer Ideas and People Sample Artistic Careers		
Animator	Graphic Designer	Photographer
Art Director	Interior Designer	Set Designer
Musician	Fashion Designer	Writer/Author

Social (Helpers) Prefer People Sample Social Careers		
Counselor	Family Therapist	Nurse
Dietitian	Probation Officer	Social Worker
Nanny	Speech Pathologist	Teacher

KICK START YOUR TEEN'S CAREER EXPLORATION 29

Enterprising (Motivators) Prefer People and Data Sample Enterprising Careers		
Entrepreneur	Chief Executive	Lawyer
Event Planner	Financial Advisor	Umpire
Judge	Real Estate Agent	Sales Agent

Conventional (Organizers) Prefer Data and Things Sample Conventional Careers		
Accountant	Compliance Officer	Office Clerk
Data Analyst	Dental Assistant	Project Manager
Librarian	Web Developer	Statistician

Now that you're beginning to understand how careers can be categorized into six types, let's involve your teen. In the upcoming chapter, your teen will have three activities to complete, which can be done in under 15 minutes. These activities are designed to gather valuable input. Upon completion, we'll assist you in analyzing their responses to identify their dominant Career Type. Then, we'll provide examples of Career Type combinations to help you pinpoint the career sectors that align with your teen's interests, allowing them to start exploring careers with purpose and direction.

CHAPTER 4
YOUR TEEN'S INPUT

It's time for your teen to take action and complete a few assessments to clarify their interests and natural tendencies. Once your teen completes the activities, the remaining chapters will help you process the results, understand and share them, and decide on the next steps with your teen. But before we dive into the assessments, let's take a moment to appreciate the power of self-reflection.

Self-reflection is a valuable tool in the journey of career exploration. It allows us to pause and examine our thoughts, feelings, and experiences, providing insights to guide us. Consider this: as your teen reflects on their interests, strengths, and goals, they're not just completing assessments—they're gaining a deeper understanding of themselves. They are defining interests and talents and envisioning options for the future. This self-awareness and introspection are the foundation of successful career planning.

Like this book, the assessments for your teen serve as a starting point, not a complete roadmap for their career journey. Our goal is to kick-start the process. Trying to tackle all aspects of career planning at once is overwhelming. Taking small, productive steps builds confidence and career planning momentum in your teen. Encourage them to take their time, explore the reasons behind their answers, and give sincere effort. Genuine responses are critical for accurate Work Style and Career Type identification.

Use your intuition to gauge their enthusiasm; some may dive in eagerly, while others may need encouragement. If your teen needs a little motivation, offer to combine the assessments with an enjoyable activity, complete them with friends, or turn them into a family affair.

A downloadable PDF of the activities is available here:
https://tinyurl.com/y7662mxt

TEEN ACTIVITIES TO COMPLETE

Congratulations! Whoever asked you to complete these activities cares about you and wants to help you figure out what comes next. These activities are short and ask you about YOU. They will help you understand yourself better and narrow down career paths to explore or reaffirm your current plan.

Before we begin, it's important to understand that in these activities, we ask you to reflect on your current self rather than who you aspire to be. Understanding your present identity provides a clearer picture of your interests and natural tendencies. This way, we can offer guidance and advice that aligns with who you are right now to help you plan your next steps. Complete these activities in a way that you can share with whomever gave them to you i.e. write on the worksheet/book, text, or email your answers. Tell me about 15 minutes to complete the three activities that follow.

Activity #1—My Thoughts

Answering the following questions helps put you in a reflective mindset and provides information that will be helpful in making connections between interests and careers.

- Name a few careers or industries you think may be a good fit for you and why.

    _____

    _____

    _____

    _____

- What careers or industries have others suggested would be a good fit for you? If you know why they made these suggestions, include that as well.

    _____

    _____

    _____

    _____

- Are there careers or industries that you know you would not enjoy? If so, list a few and why.

  _____

  _____

  _____

  _____

- Did or do you use any career exploration programs in high school? Some examples are Major Clarity, Xello, Career Cruising, Naviance, and O'Net. If so, give a summary of what you remember.

  _____

  _____

  _____

  _____

Activity #2—My Perspective

Now, when it comes to work and completing tasks, we all have personal preferences. These preferences can be called Work Styles, which revolve around a preference for working with people, data, ideas, or things. As you embark on Activity #2, it's helpful to consider why understanding your Work Style matters.

Your Work Style influences how you approach tasks, collaborate with others, and derive satisfaction from your work. You can identify career paths that resonate with your natural inclinations by recognizing your preferences in working with people, data, ideas, or things. This self-awareness can guide you toward roles where you're more likely to feel fulfilled and motivated. Let's break it down:

- **PEOPLE:** Some of us are naturally drawn to working with and helping others.
- **DATA:** Others among us are more inclined toward working with data and information.
- **IDEAS:** Then there are those who are all about creativity and innovation.
- **THINGS:** Additionally, there are people who prefer working with their hands and physical objects.

Write down the two Work Styles that you are drawn to:

#1 _____

#2 _____

Recognizing your Work Style can help you discover careers that align with how you are naturally wired. When you do work that resonates with your Work Style, you're more likely to feel fulfilled and motivated.

Activity #3—What Fits Me Best

We all have our own strengths, abilities, and interests. For example, do you have a heart for helping others? Are you organized? Do you like building or fixing things? Well, imagine that there are only six types of people in the world and that we are each a unique blend. By ranking the types from most like you to least like you, you'll gain insight into the types of careers and tasks to explore and to the careers and tasks that may not bring you joy or satisfaction.

Your job is to read each of these types and rank them in order from one to six. Number one is the most like you, and number six is the least like you. Don't worry if no one type is a perfect description of you. Do your best to rank them from most like you to least like you.

_____ **Realistic:** Enjoys work that is action-oriented and results-driven. Often described as practical, independent, persistent, and honest. Likes to work with things. Can gain energy from active, hands-on work.

_____ **Investigative:** Enjoys work that involves investigating, gathering, and analyzing information to solve problems. Often described as knowledgeable. Likes to work with things and ideas. Can gain energy from working alone.

_____ **Artistic:** Enjoys work that involves self or other types of expression. Often described as innovative, creative, and independent. Likes to work with ideas and people. Can gain energy from unstructured environments and freedom.

_____ **Social:** Enjoys helping, teaching, coaching, or caring for people. Often described as kind. Prefers to work with people. Includes introverts and extroverts. Can gain energy from assisting others.

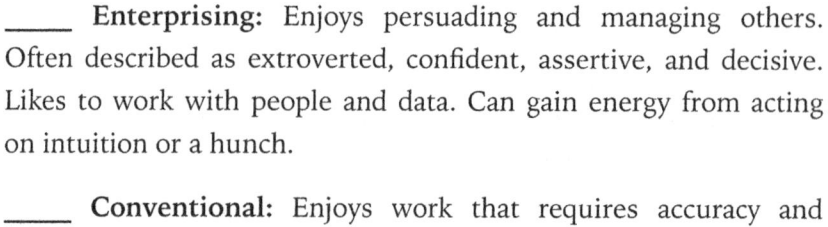

_____ **Enterprising:** Enjoys persuading and managing others. Often described as extroverted, confident, assertive, and decisive. Likes to work with people and data. Can gain energy from acting on intuition or a hunch.

_____ **Conventional:** Enjoys work that requires accuracy and attention to detail. Often described as responsible, neat, and organized. Likes to work with data and numbers. Can gain energy from seeing tasks to completion.

These six types also transfer to the world of work. Just like people are a blend of types, so are jobs. When your work aligns with your interests, it leads to greater job satisfaction, motivation, and joy. Think about this: When you talk to someone who loves their job, you often hear things like "I get to help people," "I solve problems," or "I can be innovative."

You have completed all the activities. Life is busy, and career exploration might not be your top priority right now. Not to worry; you have someone in your life who is here to help.

After you return your completed work to the person who provided it, they will process your information and assist you in interpreting your results. The goal is to help narrow in on a few career paths to explore or reaffirm your current plan.

When they discuss your results with you, remember to stay open to possibilities and be curious while sharing your thoughts and aspirations. Think of the results you receive as a compass—something pointing you in a direction, not a map dictating a destination. We aim to help you connect your natural interests and tendencies to a few careers to explore.

With thanks and appreciation, give this book back to the person who provided it to you.

CHAPTER 5
PROCESSING YOUR TEEN'S INPUT

It's time to take your teen's information and determine their individual Career Type. Don't worry about interpreting the results as you process their information. We'll do that in the next chapter.

Step One:

Review **Activity #1 (My Thoughts).** Your teen answered a series of questions. Recognizing that many teens use electronic formats, they were instructed to answer the questions simply in a way they can share them with you. This may mean you receive a long text message, email, or a typed or written document. Simply conversing with you about the questions is also perfectly acceptable. There is nothing to record, but this information is valuable to remember as we proceed.

Step Two:

Review **Activity #2 (My Preferences)** and record your teen's top two Work Style Preferences (working with PEOPLE, DATA, THINGS, or IDEAS).

#1 _____

#2 _____

Step Three:

Record the rankings from **Activity #3 (What Fits Me Best).** Your teen ranked the Career Types from one to six, with one being what fits them best.

_____ **Realistic:** Enjoys work that is action-oriented and results-driven. Often described as practical, independent, persistent, and honest. Likes to work with things. Can gain energy from active, hands-on work.

_____ **Investigative:** Enjoys work that involves investigating, gathering, and analyzing information to solve problems. Often described as knowledgeable. Likes to work with things and ideas. Can gain energy from working alone.

_____ **Artistic:** Enjoys work that involves self or other types of expression. Often described as innovative, creative, and independent. Likes to work with ideas and people. Can gain energy from unstructured environments and freedom.

_____ **Social:** Enjoys helping, teaching, coaching, or caring for people. Often described as kind. Prefers to work with people. Includes introverts and extroverts. Can gain energy from assisting others.

_____ **Enterprising:** Enjoys persuading and managing others. Often described as extroverted, confident, assertive, and decisive. Likes to work with people and data. Can gain energy from acting on intuition or a hunch.

_____ **Conventional:** Enjoys work that requires accuracy and attention to detail. Often described as responsible, neat, and organized. Likes to work with data and numbers. Can gain energy from seeing tasks to completion.

Place the first letter of your teen's first, second, and third Career Type matches in the boxes in order.

Together, these three letters are your teen's Career Type code. The code reflects not only their dominant type but also their supporting types. The types are key to kick-starting your teen's career exploration because, as we discussed in earlier chapters, jobs are categorized and easily explored by Career Types.

IMPORTANT NOTE: Your teen's preferred Career Types act as a compass, not a map. Compasses point you in a general direction, while a map gives you directions to a destination. Remember, our goal is to help you guide your teen to potential careers and pathways that, based on their input, are an informed place to start their exploration.

As you proceed through the remainder of the book, keep your teen's Career Type code and other input in mind. This will help you better understand how the results can inform their exploration and confirm why there are certain career paths that may not be a great fit. Additionally, it can be fun to have your teen rank how they feel the career types fit you. This will deepen understanding and spark great conversation.

REFLECTION AND SUPPORT

"Letting your kids grow up is kind of like releasing a kite. You hate to see it go, but it looks so beautiful and free as it climbs higher and higher in the bright blue sky."

SUSAN GALE

Dear Reader,

Before we proceed, we ask for your input.

We hope you are finding this book informative and helpful in guiding your teen toward self-awareness and informed career exploration. Your feedback is valuable to us and other parents seeking guidance.

Would you pause and take a moment right now to share your thoughts on the book by leaving a review on Amazon? Reviews matter, and your review will help other parents find this book and support their teens.

Sincere appreciation to you!

Just scan the QR code or follow the link to leave your review!

https://www.amazon.com/review/create-review/?asin=B0CW3JMHDL

CHAPTER 6
CAREER TYPE PROFILES

Think back to the analogy of career exploration being like a funnel—a world of possibilities at the wide top and career direction at the narrow bottom. Understanding and using Career Types moves us down this funnel. The types become a simplified way to find career pathways that fit a person's natural tendencies and interests.

You figured out your teen's three-letter Career Type. As a reminder, each letter represents the first letter of one of the six types. For instance, S-E-C signifies Social, Enterprising, and Conventional. We identify three types because we are a combination of types, and the letters reflect this blend. Proceed through the rest of this book with your teen's three-letter Career Type in mind. Note that the first letter is your teen's dominant type—or strongest match.

Use the note pages in the back of the book or keep a paper or device handy to jot down thoughts, questions, and items to share with your teen as you continue. Next are profiles of each type. There is insight to be gained from understanding the types that match your teen and recognizing why certain types **don't** fit. These profiles were adapted from O*NET (2023).

R - REALISTIC (DOERS)

This list is not exhaustive but aims to provide insights into characteristics and careers that fit this Career Type.

Key Words to Describe the Realistic Type		
Active	Resourceful	Build
Down to Earth	Mechanical	Drive
Hands-On	Machines	Install
Practical	Electronics	Maintain
Stable	Plants/Animals	Repair

Common Realistic Pathways
Agriculture/Natural Resources
Manufacturing and Production
Skilled Trades/Construction

Sample Realistic Careers + Code
Carpenter (RCI)
Commercial Pilot (RIE)
Computer Support Specialist (RIC)
Electrician (RIC)
Civil Engineer (RIC)
Firefighter (RSE)
Fish and Game Warden (RI)
Forester (RIE)
Mechanic Auto/Farm Equipment (RCI)
Radiological or Surgical Tech (RSC)
Welder (RCI)

If this Career Type aligns with your interests, explore it further; otherwise, feel confident not to pursue it for now.

I - INVESTIGATIVE (EXPLORERS)

This list is not exhaustive but aims to provide insights into characteristics and careers that fit this Career Type.

Key Words to Describe the Investigative Type		
Analytical	Facts	Observe
Curious	Ideas	Analyze
Insightful	Knowledge	Diagnose
Intellectual	Science	Discover
Logical	Research	Problem Solve

Common Investigative Pathways
Healthcare and Medicine
Engineering and Technology
Science and Research

Sample Investigative Careers + Code
Software Developer (ICR)
Dietitian/Nutritionist (IS)
General Medicine Physician (ISR)
Chemist (IRC)
Economist (ICE)
Mechanical Engineer (IRC)
Psychologist (Clinical) (ISA)
Audiologist (ISC)
Scientist (Multiple Industries) (I)
Urban Planner (IEA)
Penetration Tester (ICR)

If this Career Type aligns with your interests, explore it further; otherwise, feel confident not to pursue it for now.

A - ARTISTIC (CREATORS)

This list is not exhaustive but aims to provide insights into characteristics and careers that fit this Career Type.

Key Words to Describe the Artistic Type		
Creative	Sensitive	Create
Expressive	Arts	Design
Imaginative	Expression	Perform
Impulsive	Media	Self-Express
Original	Music	Write

Common Artistic Pathways
Communication
Creative Arts and Design
Media and Entertainment

Sample Artistic Careers + Code
Actor/Actress (AE)
Architect (AI)
Cosmetologist (AES)
Craft Artist (ARE)
Desktop Publisher (AIC)
Graphic Designer (ARE)
Interior Designer (AE)
Music Director/Composer (AES)
News Reporter and Journalist (AEI)
Photographer (AR)
Video Game Designer (AE)

If this Career Type aligns with your interests, explore it further; otherwise, feel confident not to pursue it for now.

S - SOCIAL (HELPERS)

This list is not exhaustive but aims to provide insights into characteristics and careers that fit this Career Type.

Key Words to Describe the Social Type		
Caring	Advise	Interact
Cooperative	Educate	Nurture
Friendly	Guide	Health
Helpful	Help	People
Kind	Communicate	Service

Common Social Pathways
Education, Teaching, and Training
Healthcare and Mental Health
Social Services

Sample Social Careers + Code
Arbitrator/Mediator (SE)
Clergy (SEA)
Community Organizer (SE)
Massage Therapist (SR)
Mental Health Counselor (SIA)
Physical Therapist (SIR)
Probation Officer (SEC)
Registered Nurse (SIC)
School Teacher (SAC)
Speech-Language Pathologist (SC)
Training Specialist (SAC)

If this Career Type aligns with your interests, explore it further; otherwise, feel confident not to pursue it for now.

E - ENTERPRISING (MOTIVATORS)

This list is not exhaustive but aims to provide insights into characteristics and careers that fit this Career Type.

Key Words to Describe the Enterprising Type		
Assertive	Ambitious	Business
Competitive	Negotiate/Sell	Customers
Confident	Lead	Employees
Optimistic	Manage	Plans
Persuasive	Market	Products

Common Enterprising Pathways
Business and Entrepreneurship
Sales and Marketing
Leadership and Management

Sample Enterprising Careers + Code
Human Resources Specialist (ECS)
Chefs and Head Cooks (ERA)
Event Planner (ECS)
Financial Advisor (ECS)
Fraud Examiner/Investigator (EIC)
Lawyers (EI)
Manager-multiple industries (ES)
Police Officer (ERS)
Producers and Directors (EAS)
Public Relations Specialist (EAS)
Real Estate Agent (EC)

If this Career Type aligns with your interests, explore it further; otherwise, feel confident not to pursue it for now.

C - CONVENTIONAL (ORGANIZERS)

This list is not exhaustive but aims to provide insights into characteristics and careers that fit this Career Type.

Key Words to Describe the Conventional Type		
Logical	Accurate	Inspect
Neat	Detailed	Information
Organized	Structured	Office
Reliable	Sort	Procedures
Responsible	Verify	Records

Common Conventional Pathways
Administrative Office Support
Finance and Accounting
Information Technology
Sample Conventional Careers + Code
Accountant/Auditor (CEI)
Administrative Assistant (CE)
CNC Tool Programmer (CIR)
Database Administrator (CI)
Dental or Surgical Assistant (CRS)
Document Management Specialist (C)
Information Security Analyst (CIR)
Logistics Analysts (CEI)
Paralegal (CER)
Quality Control Inspector (CIR)
Web Developer (CI)

If this Career Type aligns with your interests, explore it further; otherwise, feel confident not to pursue it for now.

CHAPTER 7
CAREER TYPES IN ACTION

Teens frequently find it easy to connect with and see themselves reflected in their dominant Career Type. Meet Jordan, a high school graduate with a dominant Career Type of (R) Realistic. Jordan has always enjoyed hands-on activities, whether building model airplanes or working on car engines. With her dominant type in mind, Jordan explored careers such as automotive technician, construction worker, and electrician. Ultimately, she found a strong connection with becoming an electrician, where she could put her hands-on skills to good use.

Consider the following three questions based on the profile of your teen's dominant Career Type:

1. What keywords from the profile describe your teen's actions, motivations, and interests?
2. Do the **types** of careers or pathways on the profile align with your teen's personality?
3. Are there careers or pathways on the profile that connect with hobbies, activities, or school subjects your teen enjoys?

The second letter in your teen's Career Type is their secondary type. Here is an example: Meet Maria, a high school student with a Career Type of A-S-I indicating Artistic, Social, and Investigative. Maria has always been drawn to Artistic activities like drawing, painting, and music. Maria also has a heart for helping others. After reviewing the profile of her secondary type of Social, Maria was drawn to the helping professions. She discovered art and music therapy and decided to learn more. This gave her a better understanding of how her interests and natural tendencies align with different careers and how her Career Types can be combined to explore careers and pathways that suit her.

Consider the following three questions based on the profile of your teen's secondary Career Type:

1. What keywords describe your teen's actions, motivations, and interests?
2. Are there careers or pathways on the profile that connect with hobbies, activities, or school subjects your teen enjoys?
3. How strong is the match with their secondary type versus their dominant Career Type?

Another way to explore is through the predictable relationships the Career Types have with one another. Envision a circle with the letters R, I, A, S, E, and C evenly spaced clockwise around the inside of the circle, creating a seamless flow. Here is an illustration:

```
    I   A
R  Career   S
   Type
   Relationships
    C   E
```

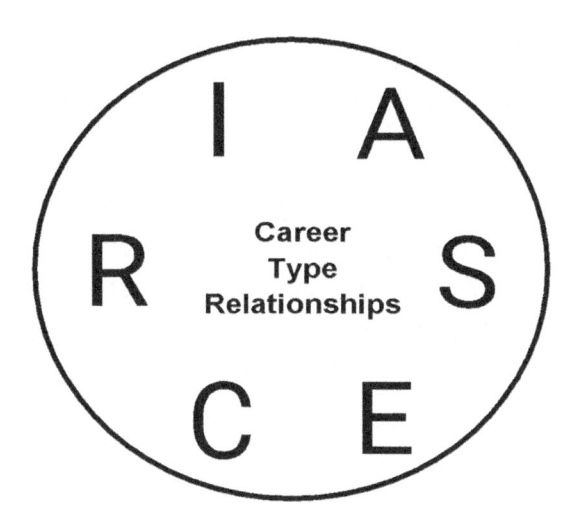

You can refer to this illustration as we explain how Career Types relate to one another.

Neighboring Career Types are those located next to each other based on the R-I-A-S-E-C order. For instance, Investigative (I) and Realistic (R) are next to one another in the circle.

Because neighboring types share similar traits, they can reveal potential career paths that align with your teen's interests beyond their dominant type. This broader perspective can help you and your teen discover additional career options. Explore the Career Types on each side of your teen's dominant type, even if those types are not one of their three letters.

Here is an example of how exploring neighboring types can help teens find a match. With a dominant Career Type of Conventional (C), Scott excels in structured environments. He enjoys organizing information and is detail-oriented. Career options such as accounting, data analysis, and quality control specialist immediately resonated with his structured and organized nature. Scott also explored the neighboring career types of Realistic (R) and

Enterprising (E). This exploration led him to discover construction management - an Enterprising (E) career with Conventional (C) traits.

We can also learn by exploring **Opposite Career Types**. These are the types on opposite sides of the R-I-A-S-E-C circle. These types showcase traits that starkly contrast one another. For instance, Conventional (C) and Artistic (A) are considered opposites. Conventional individuals tend to be highly logical and organized, while Artistic individuals lean towards creativity and impulsiveness.

Reflect on the Conventional and Artistic people in your life; you'll likely observe stark differences in their actions, reactions, and interests. Encouraging your teen to evaluate the Career Type opposite to their dominant type can provide valuable insights into their natural tendencies.

Many teens initially explore their opposite type and conclude that it doesn't align with them at all. However, finding what doesn't fit can surprisingly boost their confidence in career exploration. It's a realization that they possess a deeper understanding of the career pathways that genuinely resonate with them than they might have initially acknowledged.

We are all unique. A few teens find that they fit in both of their opposite types. Your teen may even have a three-letter Career Type that includes opposites. Usually, one of the two types will be dominant, and the opposite type will be appealing. For example, radiology combines the opposite types of Realistic and Social. It is a hands-on career that uses machines while working and interacting with people.

As you explore your teen's unique profile, consider the chapter's examples to embrace a broad perspective. Exploring neighboring types, opposite types, and the potential blending of types can be enlightening. This journey is not about finding a single answer but about helping you and your teen learn more about how their interests and natural tendencies can inform career exploration.

It's common to find undecided students with a relatively equal blend of a few Career Types instead of one dominant type. By nature, this makes it harder to narrow down a career path because there are so many paths in which they could find joy and fulfillment. While it can be frustrating, many teens take comfort in discovering that their indecision is not a lack of motivation but rather a reflection of their broad range of interests and flexibility. Those choosing to go to college can take introductory courses to learn more about options within different Career Types. Examples are Introduction to Business and Introduction to Computers. Those not attending college can do this same exploration with the jobs they choose. Teens must be reminded that they are not making one career decision for the rest of their lives. They are deciding on their next steps.

CHAPTER 8
GUIDING YOUR TEEN INTO ACTION

As we dive into the final chapter of this book, I want to emphasize the pivotal role you play. You've invested time and energy into learning a few career coaching strategies and discovering your teen's three-letter Career Type. Now, it's time to translate this knowledge into actionable steps to guide your teen toward promising careers or pathways to explore.

First and foremost, it's essential to understand that you shouldn't try to teach your teen everything you've learned in this book. Some of you will want to do just that, and we strongly encourage you to refrain.

What you've learned is intended to help you help your teen understand how to connect their interests and preferences to their career search. If you try to teach them everything you've learned, many teens will lose interest before you get to the heart of what you're after. Remember, the goal is to help your teen narrow down to two to three careers or pathways to explore, not understand career coaching strategies.

The following steps can help you guide your teen:

1. Begin a conversation with your teen about the goal of narrowing in on a few pathways to explore.

2. Have your teen read the short descriptions of the Career Types and identify what initially fits them best. Don't use your teen's three-letter Career Type or the Career Profiles from Chapter Six yet. We first want a basic introduction to the six Career Types.

> **Realistic:** Practical individuals who excel in hands-on work involving physical activity and tools.
>
> **Investigative:** Analytical people who thrive on research and problem-solving.
>
> **Artistic:** Creative souls who express themselves through artistic endeavors.
>
> **Social:** Empathetic people who find fulfillment in helping and working with others.
>
> **Enterprising:** Motivated and persuasive individuals who thrive in risk-taking and leadership roles.
>
> **Conventional:** Detail-oriented people who excel in structured and organized environments.

3. Based only on the brief descriptions above, ask questions like, "What Career Type seems to fit you best?" And "What Career Type is least like you?"

4. Share the results of the activities your teen completed. Include their three-letter Career Type and have them read the Career Type profiles from Chapter Six. This is where we help your teen better understand the Career Types and how each type ties to specific careers and pathways.

5. Encourage open and honest discussion with your teen to express their thoughts, including surprises and insights from reading the Career Type profiles.

6. Ask which Career Type profiles sparked the most enthusiasm or felt like a good fit.

7. Share your thoughts and insights and discuss their comments from Activity #1 (My Thoughts).

8. Help your teen decide on two or three careers or career pathways to explore. Please note that some teens will want to explore their Career Types further. They can read this book or search the internet using the names of the different Career Types.

After your teen has chosen a few pathways or careers to explore, they enter the "Do" phase of the motto "Explore. Plan. Do." This phase is often challenging for many teens, so it's essential to establish a clear timeframe for completion and discuss specific tasks. Agreeing on when and what needs to be accomplished can provide structure and motivation. Additionally, consider having a conversation about the level of support your teen desires from you during this process. While some teens may be eager to start, others might benefit from more encouragement and assistance. Understanding your teen's needs will help create a more effective and supportive exploration journey.

Here are six suggestions for your teen to learn more about the careers or pathways they decided to explore:

1. Research online. Some prompts include:

- How to become a (list a career).

- Careers in... (search a specific pathway)
- Typical personality for careers in (list a pathway).

2. Research the training required for careers of interest. This may guide academic choices and plans.

3. Many social media platforms provide opportunities to follow industry experts and companies in your career pathway(s) of interest. You can learn from their posts, ask questions, watch videos, and subscribe to their content. **Be bold and send a question or request to connect to discuss careers.**

4. Talk with people in your desired career or industry. Career interviews are a valuable tool for gaining perspective. These informal conversations offer insights into daily work, challenges, joys, and training requirements. You can learn things from these interviews that you will not find online. Explore, ask questions, and make connections.

Here is a list of Career Interview questions you might ask:

- "What initially attracted you to this career?" This helps you understand their initial motivations.
- "Did you have a straight path into this career?" Learning their history helps describe their journey.
- "Can you share something surprising about your day-to-day work?" This helps you discover lesser-known facts.
- "What are the most rewarding aspects of your job?" Asking this usually identifies a value or motivation.
- "What's one unexpected aspect of your job that you wish you'd known earlier?" This question can lead anywhere.
- "Describe the type of person who excels in this career." Answers to this question often match the characteristics of specific Career Types.

A word of caution. The interview results will differ based on whether the person enjoys their work. You can often determine job satisfaction during the interview. If you interview someone who is unsatisfied with their job, listen for the reasons for the dissatisfaction. The reasons are often tied to a mismatch between a person's career type, values, needs, or skills.

5. Use the career exploration programs available through your school or local library.

6. Talk with the person who had you complete the activities in this book, your school counselor, a coach, a family friend, etc. Talking with others gives you a place to process your thoughts and assists in learning about yourself and deciding on your next steps.

A CLOSING MESSAGE TO PARENTS

Parents, as you guide and support your teen through this crucial phase, remember that every path is unique, and it's okay if your teen's career journey differs from what you had envisioned. Pursuing a career that aligns with their interests is just one key to long-term career satisfaction. This book has provided the foundation, a kick start, if you will, to their career exploration journey.

If this book has ignited understanding and motivation in your teen —fantastic! For those who seek more in-depth assistance or have a teen resistant to parental guidance (which is quite common), don't hesitate to contact a career counselor, career advisor, career navigator, or myself at amyzcareerguidance@yahoo.com. We are here to help.

This is the first part of the journey. As you and your teen take these steps forward, remember that the path to a fulfilling career is filled with discovery and growth. Embrace it with enthusiasm, curiosity, and JOY!

HERE'S A CHANCE TO HELP OTHER PARENTS

By sharing a review of this book on Amazon, you'll help other parents like you kick start their teen's career exploration.

We thank you so much for your support and wish your teen every success on their journey.

TAKE A MOMENT TO SHARE YOUR THOUGHTS!
LEAVE US A REVIEW TO BENEFIT OTHERS JUST LIKE YOU

Just scan the QR code or follow the link to leave your review!

https://www.amazon.com/review/create-review/?asin=B0CW3JMHDL

The End

REFERENCES

O*NET 28.0 Database (https://www.onetcenter.org/database.html) by the U.S. Department of Labor, Employment and Training Administration (USDOL/ETA). It is used under the CC BY 4.0 license. O*NET® is a trademark of USDOL/ETA. Author Amy Zdanowski has modified all or some of this information. USDOL/ETA has not approved, endorsed, or tested these modifications.

"Forty of the Most Inspiring, Heartfelt Quotes About Raising Teens." Parentingteensandtweens.com. Last modified February 26, 2023. https://parentingteensandtweens.com/forty-of-the-most-inspiring-heartfelt-quotes-about-raising-teens/.

NOTES

Made in United States
Orlando, FL
05 September 2024